[THE BOOK]

By Rick Stacy
& Jamie Wetzel

ISBN: 1467996467
ISBN-13:978-1467996464

DEDICATION

To the people of God at Meridian Christian Church
and to our Lord Jesus Christ.

CONTENTS

ACKNOWLEDGMENTS

This book is the result of a teaching series at Meridian Christian Church. It was originally taught in the fall of 2011.

We (Rick and Jamie) want to thank John Datema (MCC Family Life Minister) and Tyler Sherman (MCC Youth Minister) for their time and insights as we worked on these messages in our teaching team meetings each week.

A LOOK AT THE BOOK

"For whatever was written in former days was written for our instruction, that through endurance and through the encouragement of the Scriptures we might have hope."

Romans 15:4 (ESV)

Bible = Book. It comes from the Latin word *biblia*. Literally the word means book. The Bible is THE BOOK. It is the book of the ages because of what it is – a collection of writings that reveal the nature of God and his interaction with man. It was written over 1600 years – over 60 Generations – and there is nothing like it in all of human history.

A scholar was asked to create a list of 50 great books of western civilization. Then he was asked if these 50 books, written over the space of several centuries, agreed with and were in harmony with each other. The answer, of course, was that these books were a conglomeration of distinctly different thoughts, teachings, and philosophies of life. There was no harmony what so ever.

In contrast, the Bible is a harmony of truth that was revealed by God to men through men. Moreover the Bible has survived and is still held in high esteem by men and women all over the planet in spite of the passage of thousands of years, waves of persecution, and all manner of criticism – both of the content and of the authorship.

When you watch a special about the Bible on the Discovery Channel it is usually critical of the book. The amazing thing to me is that they present arguments as new when the objections they raise are as old as the Bible itself. People have attempted to discredit the Bible for as long as it has existed. And yet, here are all the old arguments again – new and just recently discovered. Simply put, the criticisms raised in these TV shows are not new!

The fact is that over the centuries, the Bible has been vetted, tested, analyzed, criticized, reviewed, and examined by literally thousands of scholars since the first word was recorded. There is no writing on earth in all of history that has been as carefully and thoroughly scrutinized by friend and enemy alike… and yet it holds up to this day as the most influential book of all time.

I want to touch on just two areas to consider and understand when you begin to look at [THE BOOK.]

First, we'll look at both the Old Testament and New Testament canon. We'll look at why the books in the list were included while others were not.

Second, we'll look at the languages and the translations of the Bible. There are many and it can be a bit confusing unless you understand the differences.

The Canon

Let's begin with the writings. You might want to think of the canon as the table of contents.

So, how did the list of writings that make up [THE BOOK] come into being? Who decided? What is scripture and what is not? This is an important question and one that has been examined over the centuries – repeatedly throughout history and in recent days.

To answer the question we have to look at the two main sections of the Bible separately because each came into existence differently. These two main sections are called the Old Testament and the New Testament.

A testament is a statement or document that the author has sworn to be true. It is a testimony to the truth. When you write a will it is called a testament because you swear it to be a true expression of your wishes upon your death.

This book claims to be a true testimony from God, about God, about us, the reason for our existence, and our ultimate end. This is a testimony about the truth of life. You don't have to climb a mountain and find a hermit in a cave to learn the secret of life. It is in [THE BOOK].

The first testament, (The Old Testament) is a collection of writings about the people of Israel. In this testament we are told that God has chosen to reveal himself to all of humanity – whom He created – through the descendants of one man because of his standing before God and because of his faith. That man is Abraham.

This testament is a collection of historical, prophetic, and poetic writings that tell about and surround the story of God's interaction through four promises to four different men – Noah, Abraham, Moses, and David. As I have studied about these four important promises of the Old Testament – to Noah, Abraham, Moses, and David, I have been amazed at the level of harmony that is the Bible.

The OT Canon is a collection of writings by the people who were part of that history and prophesy over the years. The people of Israel knew the authors and respected their voice. They revered the words, protected and died for them.

The OT Canon

The arrangement of the original list as kept by the Hebrew people was different than ours is today. The writings are the same – it is just the arrangement that is different.

The reason for this is quite simple. These writings were done on scrolls made from papyrus. Papyrus is made from a reed that was soaked and beaten into an ancient form of paper. Rather than made into pages and then bound up in a book like we do, the ancients fashioned a scroll of paper as wide as necessary. Then they would pile the scrolls into sections according to the subject matter and place them into clay pots for protection from the elements.

They were kept and protected as the writings of the people of Israel.

The Law (Torah)

Written by Moses, who was trained in Egypt, the law is a compilation of five scrolls. These scrolls tell the story of the beginning of man, the beginning of a chosen people, and the establishment of the Old Covenant law with those people through Moses. They are:

Genesis
Exodus
Leviticus
Numbers
Deuteronomy

The Former Prophets

Joshua
Judges
Samuel
Kings

The Latter Prophets

Isaiah
Jeremiah
Ezekiel
The Twelve

The Writings

Poetry
Psalms
Proverbs
Job

Five Rolls (Megilloth)

Song of Songs
Ruth
Lamentations
Esther
Ecclesiastes
Historical
Daniel
Ezra-Nehemiah

The New Testament Canon

The New Testament contains documents concerning the coming of a new promise through God himself who appeared among us. This is Jesus, the one who was promised in the Old Testament and who is the Messiah.

So how were these writings selected from all the writings concerning Jesus? There were many. If you have been listening you have probably heard about the gospel of Thomas and the Apocrypha as well as many other writings. Dan Brown in his fictional novels has made much of secret writings that reveal new truths.

They are not new. These new truths are old lies that have been around for centuries and known by many scholars. They were rejected centuries ago for good reason.

The writings that have become part of the NT Canon were established and set with in the first couple of generations of the life of Christ. They were recognized in later centuries – but not chosen just collected into one codex – The Bible.

There were five guiding principles for inclusion in the NT Canon

Is the writing Authoritative?

That is, does it purport to be a revealing of truth from the hand of God?

Is it Prophetic?

"Prophetos" is a compound word that means literally "to speak forth" or to speak out with power. In other words, prophesy is not to be relegated to "future telling" but it is preaching or speaking out the truth about God. That is, is this writing a powerful speaking forth about God by a man of God?

Is it Authentic?

Is the authorship verified? Is it truthful and correct? Was it written where and when it was supposed to have been? Did others who knew the author verify its authenticity? The early church fathers had a policy of rejecting any writing that was doubtful in any way.

Is it Dynamic?

This is subjective but to be included in the canon of the NT the church as a whole had to (by consensus) accept that this writing had transforming power. People who read the testimony were moved and dynamically affected. In other words, did the writing have the life-transforming power of God?

Was it received, collected, read and used?

Perhaps the most important guiding principle was the general acceptance of the writing. Was it widely circulated, read, shared, and understood by the church as a testimony that spoke of the truth of God?

There is a teaching today that the canon was chosen and put together 300 years after Jesus death. That is not true. Yes, there were various counsels of church leaders in that time period and the canon was recognized and published. These counsels merely recognized the reality of what the church had already established and accepted as the authoritative list of gospels, history, letters, and prophesies from the teachings of the apostles.

The Bible Today

Today the Bible list has been standardized. You can thank the scholars who translated and published the King James Version back in the 1600's for our present arrangement of these writings.

The arrangement of the canon we have in our Bibles today is listed below. This is how I learned it:

Old Testament

Law (Early History – 5)
Israelite History (History – 12)
Poetry (Poetry – 5)
Major Prophets (Prophesy – 5)
Minor Prophets (Prophesy – 12)

New Testament

Gospels (Biography – 4)
Acts (History – 1)
Letters (To churches, Individuals and all believers – 21)
Revelation (Apocalyptic writings – 1)

Bible Languages, Translations, and Versions

The Bible is the most carefully scrutinized, criticized, analyzed, and examined writing in the entire history of human kind. We can be confident that what we have is what was originally written.

The Original Languages

The original languages of the Old Testament were Hebrew and Aramaic. The New Testament was written in Greek.

The First Translations

The first Old Testament translation was called the "Septuagint." This was a Greek translation authorized by the Roman Emperor and was done at the library of Alexandria in Egypt. This Greek version of the Hebrew text was translated in about 160 BC. The Latin Vulgate was the Latin (Roman) translation of both the Old and the New Testaments.

From the time of the original manuscripts to the middle ages, when printed Bibles became more common, these sacred writings were carefully copied by hand. Whole communities of monks and scribes devoted their lives to copying the Bible letter by letter and word by word. Since they believed that these were the revelation of a loving God they made sure that every word and every mark was painstakingly reproduced.

After the time of hand copied scrolls and codex's (leather bound hand copied books) the Bible gave way to printed books. The Guttenberg Bible, the first printed with movable type, was an edition of the Latin Vulgate.

Very soon there began to be a variety of translations into the common languages of the people. At first these were resisted by church leaders and early translators were called heretics and some were burned at the stake. Eventually these caught on and there began to be a number of different translations.

In the early 1600's King James of England commissioned the writing of a version that became the standard for the English speaking world for almost four centuries.

By the way, the "authorized" King James Version was "authorized" by King James – not by God! He paid the scholars and commissioned the translation. It is by far one of the most influential of all translations in all time but it wasn't any more important than any of the other translations.

Many Modern Versions

In the early and middle of the 20th Century there began to be a need for a version that was easier to understand than the King James Version that was becoming archaic. The main versions during the early part of the century were the American Standard Version (ASV) and the Revised Standard (RSV). In the late 60's and early 70's two more versions became widely used. The Todays English Version (TEV), was written with a somewhat limited vocabulary while the New International Version (NIV) became and still is the standard for most evangelicals from 1970 until today.

In the 21st Century we have seen the rise of several new versions including the New Century Version (NCV) and the English Standard Version (ESV). I have recently begun to use the ESV because of the contemporary flow of the language and it's precision.

In addition to these translations there are several paraphrases that many people enjoy reading. Versions translate carefully from one language to another word for word. The better translations are done by large committees and teams who work for several years to complete the task.

A paraphrase is a "thought for thought" translation. The Living Bible (completed in the 1970's) was the work of one man (Kenneth Taylor) and so is limited to that man's understanding of the text. The Message is a modern paraphrase and is very good. It's great for reading. The most important thing to remember about a paraphrase is that they are great for general understanding but lack the exacting precision of a careful "word for word" translation.

Besides all these different versions there are many Bibles with study helps printed along with the text. When you go to the Bible Book Store you can purchase several kinds of study tools to help you get a better understanding of the Bible's message. There are study Bibles, interlinear Bibles (with both the original language and modern translation), commentaries, Bible encyclopedias, and Bible dictionaries.

Today, through the internet, there are many powerful tools available to help you read and study the Bible. Listed below are some great Bible study sights! Check them out.

Digital Bible Sites and Helps

BibleGateway.com: A searchable Bible study site with over 100 versions. They also have commentaries and devotionals available. Free!

E-Sword.net: A great source for downloadable Bible study software. They have many different Bibles, commentaries and dictionaries available in a "tiled windows" application – absolutely free. You can make a donation if you wish.

Logos.com: This software is fairly expensive but extremely powerful. Not only does it have a multitude of versions and helps but also many other books and authors are available – and it's all searchable and very useable. It's not free but it is really good.

YouVersion.com: For your smart phone one of the best options available is the YouVersion Bible. It comes with all kinds of versions and in a variety of languages with personalized reading programs, book marks and lots of other bells and whistles – and it's free!

So which should I use? Use any of them you want. Use more than one. Understand that a paraphrase is just that. The message of God will be there.

The only caveat is to stay away from any Bible version that is published and used by only one group or church. These have usually been translated to emphasize a particular teaching or doctrine – sometimes without any scholarly foundation.

Even then I have used these versions to share God's truth because it's still there!

Are you new to [The BOOK]?

So where do you start? Here is my suggestion…

John – Get to know Jesus

Acts – Learn about the beginning of the church

Romans – Understand why Jesus came (Chapters 1-8) and learn how to live for Jesus (9-16)

Action Steps

- ❑ Confess Jesus as Lord and be baptized
- ❑ Get a modern version Bible
- ❑ Start reading the Gospel of John
- ❑ Start reading every day and keep a journal
- ❑ Download a YouVersion Bible into your phone

Discussion Questions

1. When did your first start reading the Bible? What version did you use? What version do you use today? Why? How many versions are there in your group today?

2. Read Romans 15:4; 2 Timothy 3:16-17; 1 Peter 1:24-25; 2 Peter 1:20-21. What does the Bible say about its value to us as a) a culture, b) a nation, and c) individuals.

3. What is your favorite portion of scripture? Take a few minutes and either review the narrative or read the text. Why is your choice so meaningful to you?

4. How has the word of God helped you in general ways? How has it helped you in a time of stress, conflict, or decision?

OLD TESTAMENT HISTORY

The content of this Book is radical, life-changing, eternally impacting.

Most of the time, we focus on the content. Our purpose in writing this book is to focus on the context. If we don't understand the context, we can misinterpret the content. If we don't understand what style of writing we're reading, when it was written and to who, why it was written and how it fits into the theme of the entire Book, we can misinterpret it. And the content is far too important to screw up.

In this chapter we're going to focus on the Old Testament books of Historical Literature.

There are 39 books in the Old Testament: 17 Historical, 17 Prophets, and 5 Poetry. The Books of the Old Testament that we're going to focus on as Historical literature are Genesis through Esther.

They cover a period from creation to 400 BC. That's around 3,000 years. Some people complain that the Bible is long and boring but think of trying to condense 3,000 years of a nation's history into one book. It'd be tough, wouldn't it? I think God did us a favor by cutting it down to this length. I'm sure he must have said, "Take it back, it's too long!" several times.

Our goal is to provide some context for the books of Old Testament history.

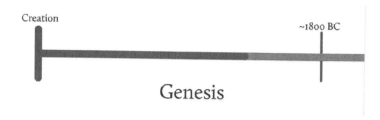

Creation

~1800 BC

Genesis

Genesis

The title "Genesis" is Latin for origin, birth, or beginning. Genesis covers from the time of creation until 1800 BC. We don't know with reliability when creation was. The earliest date that we know of with some certainty was the birth and call of Abraham, around 2100 BC.

Genesis tells the story of God's creation of a perfect world, Mans rejection of God including the stories of Adam and Eve, the fall, Cain killing Abel, and the time when every inclination of man's heart is evil.

At the flood, God starts over with Noah. Then came God's plan to reverse the effects of sin on mankind through Abraham. The rest of Genesis tells about the promises to Abraham (a great people, the promised land of Canaan, a privileged relationship with God, and a purpose-to bless the nations). Abraham has a son named Isaac, who is the father of Jacob and Esau.

Jacob (who is called "Israel" by God), has 12 sons, one of whom, Joseph, is sold into slavery in Egypt. Joseph ends up saving his family from famine by settling them in Egypt. Jacob's sons and their families grow great in numbers and become grouped into families, or "tribes of Israel," living in peace in Egypt as the book of Genesis ends.

Exodus

The title is from Greek and means "the way out." That family of words is familiar to us in English also: exit.

From 1800 BC to 1450 BC Jacob's family descendants multiplied. For a period of about 150 years, they lived peacefully, and then a Pharaoh came to power who knew nothing about Joseph. And so the Egyptians oppressed the Israelites as slaves for around 280 years. Then Moses is born (the baby in a basket), he grows up, hears God from a burning bush, and God tells him that he'll lead Israel's people out of slavery in Egypt. Moses returns to Egypt, but Pharaoh refuses to release the people, so God uses ten plagues to convince him. The people leave Egypt, via a miraculous crossing of the Red Sea. Moses goes up a mountain and God gives him the covenant on stone tablets (The Ten Commandments). Then Moses built the tabernacle as a place for God's spirit to signify that he is with them in the wilderness.

In all of this, God is bringing them out of Egypt to the land he had promised Abraham.

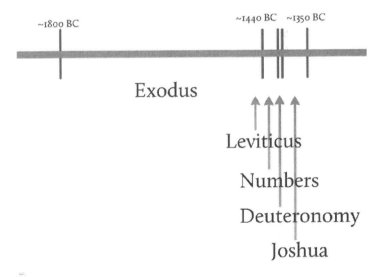

Leviticus

The title refers to the family clan of Levi, one of Jacob's 12 sons, who were designated as the tribe through which the priests of Israel would come, the go-betweens for the people of Israel and God. They would give Levitical, or priestly, instruction.

This book is typically the one we skip, and is least read. It is filled with instructions for the people that seem outdated, irrelevant, and foreign. The listings are boring and filled with crazy details.

It's important to understand what Leviticus is. Basically, the book is the legal code for a brand new nation. God is creating a nation out of a people that have been subjects, slaves, and had no say for 400-plus years. They needed some direction as to how to live and act together?

It's also designed to create a holy people, a nation set apart and unique from the other nations because it would be ruled by God. This required not just political and legal instructions, but also spiritual ones.

Numbers

The title refers to the two censuses that are taken in the book, but don't let that discourage you from reading it. Those are only in two of the 36 chapters. The rest of the book is narrative and covers the time of the Israelites from about a year after they left Egypt until they enter the Promised Land of Canaan that God is taking them to. The problem is, that journey was supposed to take a lot shorter than it did.

From the start, the people complained about lack of water, about the food God was providing them, and about Moses' leadership. Despite the display of God's power in the plagues and exodus from Egypt, the parting of the Red Sea, they constantly doubted that God would provide for them.

They came up to the edge of the Promised Land and then refused to go in! So God says Israel will wander in the desert for 40 years until that generation dies off and they wouldn't get the blessing he had prepared for them. So they wander around. After the first generation died off the people finally come back to the edge of the Promised Land and instructions were given as to how the land will be divided up by 12 tribes.

Deuteronomy

The title is from Greek meaning "second law". Moses again gives the laws and covenant regulations from Leviticus to the nation of Israel. It's called the second law because he's giving it for the second time, to the new generation, the original generation having died in the wilderness.

So they're back, about to enter the land God's giving them and Moses recaps some of the events and history over the past 40 years, and is reminding them of God's instructions to them. Moses is not just giving the laws, but pleading with them to remain committed and faithful to God. They have an incredible opportunity for a special and privileged relationship with God.

It ends with God appointing a successor to Moses, Joshua, who was to lead the people into the Promised Land. Then Moses goes up on a mountain to look over the Promised Land, and he dies there.

Joshua

The title is from the main character, Joshua, who leads the people in following God into the land he is giving them. The events take place around 1400 BC.

Remember the story of Jericho...the walls came a-tumbling down? That happens as part of the conquest of Canaan by the nation of Israel. The book of Joshua also tells how the twelve tribes of Israel, descendants of Jacob and of Abraham, settle into the land and begin to reap the blessings of God's promises.

Judges

What began so promising didn't last long. Some 20 years after Joshua's death, the nation begins to reject God. Judges describes the late 1300s BC until about 1050 BC.

As a result, God, as he stated in the covenant he made with Israel, allowed foreign nations to invade and enslave them. They would cry out to God, he would raise up a judge to deliver them from servitude, and they would enjoy a period of rest or silence. But then the cycle would happen again and again, only the depths of sin would be more and more depraved each time.

In Judges we learn about Gideon, Samson, and Deborah, and others.

Ruth

The title is the name of the main character. The book chronicles events in her life and takes place during the period of the Judges. It's a good example of how the nation was to be a blessing. Ruth was from Moab. She married an Israelite man who died, but who then followed her mother-in-law back to Israel.

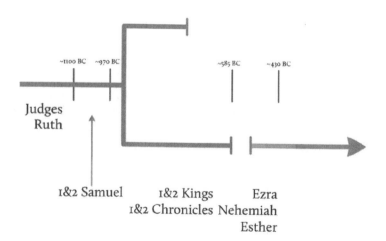

1 & 2 Samuel

These books are named after a prominent man named Samuel. They cover from 1110 BC to 970 BC, about 140 years. Samuel was the last of the Judges and the first of a new kind of prophet.

God established Israel to be a nation where he was their king, set apart and completely unique from the nations around them. They were to be an example of what it would be like if they also submitted to God as their king. Instead, they rejected God as king in Judges, and now in Samuel, they request that they want a king like all the other nations.

So God granted their request. Saul is anointed by Samuel as Israel's first king, and Israel enters into a period of being ruled by men through a monarchy.

The books of 1 and 2 Samuel cover the time of Saul and David, the first two kings. Here is where we find the stories of David and Goliath as well as David and Bathsheba.

Israel then continues the monarchy established by Saul and David. David's son Solomon becomes king. He's the one known for his wisdom. From the outside, this is the high point of Israel's power and influence in the world. But trouble was brewing on the inside. Solomon was not staying faithful to God and idolatry was gaining a foothold in the kingdom.

At Solomon's death, his son takes the throne, but he's an arrogant man, and because of him antagonizing the people, the nation rebels and effectively splits in two, in 930 BC.

What follows is a history of these two nations, focusing on a chronicling of the kings of each of these kingdoms.

The northern kingdom, made up of the territory of ten of the tribes of Israel, retains the name Israel, or Samaria. The southern kingdom, made up of the territory of two of the tribes of Israel, the largest being the territory of Judah, remains faithful to the line of David. They become known simply as Judah, and Jerusalem remains its capital.

Let's follow the northern kingdom. The capital of the former united kingdom was Jerusalem, now in the southern kingdom of Judah. So what else was in Jerusalem? The temple, and the center of the worship of Yahweh, of God. Now, the northern kingdom can't have their people continuing to travel to their adversary's capital, so they set up an alternative religion, centered in two places in the northern kingdom, which eventually became mixed with the idol worship of some of the surrounding nations.

The kings of Israel, this northern kingdom, ended up representing nine different dynasties, or family lines, of kings. If we were to describe the kings as "good" or "bad" in terms of how well they led the people in being faithful to God, every single one of the kings of the northern kingdom are described in the Bible as "bad." They "did evil in the eyes of the Lord."

As a result, God continually sent prophets to warn the northern kingdom that it needed to return to faithfulness or they would be punished. Well, this lasted around 200 years before God used a neighboring empire to enact his justice.

The Assyrian Empire at this time was the dominant world power in the area. Their capital was Nineveh, which might sound familiar to you from the story of Jonah. It is located in the north where today we have Iraq, Syria, Iran, and Turkey. They came down into Israel and in 722 BC completely conquered Israel/Samaria.

The Assyrians had developed a policy for the territories they conquered. In order to limit the chances of these territories rebelling, they would send the people into exile, taking large amounts of the population and transplanting them into other areas of their empire. So this is what they did to the northern kingdom, and then other conquered peoples from other territories were transplanted to Israel/Samaria.

What's left in this area is a population of people of mixed descent, Jewish as well as other races from around the Assyrian Empire. You take that, the idol-worship, and the false religion that has taken root, and fast-forward to Jesus' day, 700 years later. What you find is a group of people in the New Testament we know as the Samaritans. Do you see why the Jews in Jesus' day looked down on these people? They were no longer pure Jews, and they had not held to the true worship of God that Moses had helped establish.

Ok, let's go back to the Southern Kingdom, or Judah. The kingdom of Judah lasted longer than Israel, about 350 years, and the line of kings followed the lineage of King David, as God had promised. They lasted longer because they attempted to remain faithful to the covenant of Yahweh that had been established. The kings through the years were described as a mixture of good and bad kings.

However, ultimately, they too turned their back on God, despite his warnings, and God used another world power to bring about his judgment.

By then Assyria had faltered and been overcome by the Babylonians, who then destroyed the Egyptians who came to the Assyrians aid, and the Babylonian Empire began. After a few rebellions and attacks, the Babylonians conquered Judah and destroyed Jerusalem in 586 BC destroying the temple of God.

The Babylonian policy was to take the best and the brightest of the people they conquered and take them back to Babylon, where they would be indoctrinated into the Babylonian beliefs and culture. Can you think of any people from Judah who were removed and taken to Babylon? They included Daniel, Shadrach, Meschach, and Abednego.

So now we're left with the northern kingdom dispersed and no more, many of the Southern Jews in exile in Babylon, with a remnant still in Judah.

1 & 2 Kings and 1 & 2 Chronicles

1 & 2 Kings and 1 & 2 Chronicles cover the same time period, and they're essentially identical in the events they cover. The difference is their perspective. The books of Kings were written shortly after the fall of Jerusalem, and the author's purpose seems to be to reiterate to the people why they were

being punished – because they had rejected the covenant their forefathers had made with God.

The books of Chronicles, however, were written later and seek to encourage the remnant and those in exile that God was still faithful to them, and so its accounts tend to be more positive, and focus on the promise of David's line to continue.

Esra & Nehemiah

Look back at the timeline on page 18. While the Jews are in exile in Babylon, the Medo-Persian Empire conquered the Babylonians. Cyrus, the Persian conqueror, issues a decree allowing the Jews to return to their homeland, which they start doing in several different waves. A man named Zerubbabel leads the people back to Jerusalem and oversees the rebuilding of the temple there. This is covered in the book of Ezra, named after a spiritual leader who led a second group's return to Judah. A third group returns with Nehemiah, and under his leadership the walls of the city of Jerusalem are rebuilt.

Esther

The last book in our historical literature is Esther which, like the book of Ruth, is kind of a side-step book telling a side story of a woman who is one of the exiled Jews in the now-Persian empire. If you've seen the movie *300* (which I can't officially endorse), the Persian king, Xerxes, who goes to war to invade the Greek city-states, is the one who makes Esther his queen. That takes place during this period.

So this is where the Old Testament essentially ends, with the Jewish people living as subjects to whatever world power is in control. After the Persians, it's the Greeks and then the Romans, and that's the world that Jesus is born into.

Everything that happens in the Old Testament fits into the timeline of these books. The rest of the books of the OT (poetry, prophecy) deal within events narrated in the books of history.

Application

How does understanding the context of this section of the Bible aid us as we read? Here's one example: If we understand it's a historical narrative of events, we won't confuse *description* with *prescription*. We recognize that the narrators are *describing* events that are happening, but not necessarily advocating it or *prescribing* their behavior as something we should model. We wouldn't read a history book about WWII-era Germany and think that because it's written down, it's something we should do. We recognize that what we're reading is a narrative of historical events. Similarly, we can't always assume that Israel is the good guy, so they're always acting right, and we should model it.

We need to evaluate in terms of: is what they are doing giving honor to God? Understanding that it is a historical narrative helps us to better interpret the content.

So, how does understanding the context of Old Testament History help us as we read? Here's one example: understanding the context helps us see the big picture, and that helps us understand how what we're reading fits into that big picture.

The OT Historical Literature is a narrative of events, but with a purpose and an intention. Running through the Old Testament is a consistent theme: God's purpose is to reclaim the people of the world, to draw those that he loves back to a relationship with him. This means He wants to set aside a group of people as his. They will demonstrate by their lives what it's like to live under the blessings of God's rule. The rest of the world will be drawn to this. So through a small group of people set aside as unique, holy, or for a special purpose, the whole world will be blessed. Does that sound familiar? It should because it describes the church.

By understanding this, we see how the events helped to accomplish that purpose. We begin to understand the purposes of God shown in the Old Testament are not negated by the New Testament, but the New Testament is a continuation of what God's purposes and means have been all along!

Action Steps:

- ❏ Read three chapters from a book of history (Genesis through Esther).
- ❏ Read a commentary or more in-depth resource on one of the books of history.
- ❏ Join a group that is studying the Bible (Growth Group, Men's or Women's group).
- ❏ Start a regular Bible reading plan.

Discussion Questions

1. Have you read any of the 17 books of history in the OT? (Genesis to Esther) Which was (or are) your favorites and why?

2. How does understanding the historical context of a OT book help you apply lessons from the text for your life? Give an example or two.

3. How is the descriptive nature of historical writing different than prescriptive nature of the New Testament letters? How does that affect the way you read and study the OT history books?

4. How does understanding the historical context help you to see the big picture of God's purposes? How have you seen the Bible—as a collection of interesting but essentially unconnected stories or as a harmony of narratives with a common theme?

5. Give an example of a narrative in the Old Testament that reveals and points to the truth(s) of the New Testament?

PROPHECY

Let me remind you of our objective – to understand the context of what we read. Understanding the Book allows us to better understand and interpret the content of what we read.

The Books of Prophecy

Let's review the timeline–in the last chapter we covered 3000 years of history in just a few pages. The prophets in the Bible who have books named after them cover a relatively narrow period of that history, from 800 to 400 BC, around 400 years.

The Books of the Old Testament that are included as Prophecy are Isaiah through Malachi.

They are called the Major and Minor Prophets. This has nothing to do with significance, but rather the length of the book. Basically, if they talked for a long time, they got labeled as a major prophet. (Two groups of people understand this well: Politicians and Preachers. Who wants to be a minor politician?)

As we attempt to read the prophets, there are certain difficulties we encounter (Martin Luther, the 16th century reformer and theologian said, "They have a queer way of talking, like people who, instead of proceeding in an orderly manner, ramble off from one thing to the next so that you cannot make heads or tails of them or see what they are getting at.")

1. The prophetic books, especially the longer ones, are collections of spoken oracles, not always presented in their original chronological sequence, often without hints as to where one oracle ends and another begins, and often without hints as to their historical setting.

2. Most of these verbal oracles were spoken in poetry, which is obviously characterized by metaphorical and illustrative language.

3. The time period of the prophets, while relatively short in the history of Israel, is still 400 years. Think of people writing messages to us in 2011 and 1611, and how different the writing style and vocabulary would be. And they don't even write in the same style in their own day.

Reading the prophets can be challenging. But, we can't just ignore such a large chunk of the Bible that has been given to us for our growth and learning. We need to understand the prophets.

Let's start by reviewing three prominent roles in the Old Testament:

- Kings: The intent was God would fill this role, but men did. Unfortunately, they often led the people astray.
- Priests: They were the go-betweens for people and God. Unfortunately many became corrupted, and more influenced by the king's commands rather than God.
- Prophet: These were persons who God prompted to give messages to the people, the king, and the nation.

I heard someone once say that he thought of prophets like Jedi — moral watch-keepers of the people, independent of the government and somewhat mystical and mysterious. (The analogy breaks down when it comes to light sabers, though.)

Most of the time we picture them as wizards like Gandalf. We think of a Nostradamus-type figure, someone proclaiming the future. *Future-telling* is a part of Old Testament prophecy, but it is mostly *truth-telling*.

Future-telling is actually a very small portion of the content of these books. When they announced the future, it was usually the immediate future of Israel, Judah, and the surrounding nations – not our future. One of the keys to understanding the Prophets, therefore, is to stop trying to interpret them as applying to today and to focus instead on their message.

To see the prophets as primarily predictors of future events is to miss their primary function, which was, in fact, to speak for God to their contemporaries. They were God's messengers. He would speak to them, and they would speak what they heard. These were just normal people who were obeying God by communicating a message.

They communicated these messages often in creative ways. They were writers, preachers, poets, actors, but they were also normal people: husbands, fathers, young men, old men.

If anything, they were the covenant-enforcers, saying, we entered into an agreement with God (remember the promises to Abraham?) and we're not fulfilling our end of the bargain. Therefore:

- The messages that they spoke were often negative.
- They were contrary to what people wanted to hear.
- They spoke in opposition to the majority.

As a result, they were not often well-liked. Have you ever had someone in your life that when they spoke, you knew it was going to be pointing out something you needed to change? I've been on both sides of that, and it's not enjoyable.

Let's look at an overview of prophets — remember the kingdom split around 930 BC into the northern kingdom, or Israel (Samaria), and the southern kingdom, or Judah.

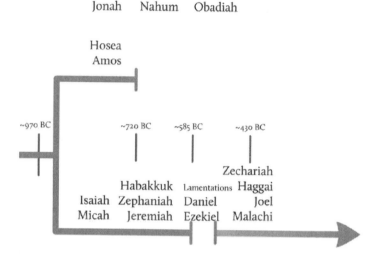

Jonah   Nahum   Obadiah

Hosea
Amos

~970 BC   ~720 BC   ~585 BC   ~430 BC

Zechariah
Habakkuk   Lamentations   Haggai
Isaiah   Zephaniah   Daniel   Joel
Micah   Jeremiah   Ezekiel   Malachi

Jonah warned Nineveh, the capital of Assyrian Empire and they repented!

Hosea and **Amos** warned the northern kingdom. They told them to repent but they didn't! The northern kingdom was destroyed by the Assyrian Empire in 722 BC.

Isaiah and **Micah** preached to the southern kingdom of Judah.

Nahum warned Nineveh, capital of Assyrian Empire, that God proclaimed their fall at the hands of the conquering Babylonian Empire.

Habakkuk, Zephaniah, and **Jeremiah** all preached to the southern kingdom warning them to repent. They didn't and were conquered by Babylonian Empire in 586 BC when they were taken into exile.

Lamentations told of the fall of Jerusalem.

Ezekiel and **Daniel** prophesied during time of exile to Babylon and the Persian Empire.

Obadiah warned Edom, a neighboring country, of the privileged relationship Israel had with God and that he would curse those who cursed his people.

Zechariah, **Haggai** and **Malachi** told of the return from exile to the land, reminding them of how they were to live.

Joel has a somewhat uncertain date because there aren't very many internal clues. He preached to Judah.

Despite the various times and places, the messages of the prophets contained pretty similar themes. I think these topics and their application are meaningful for us today as well.

1. Sin

This was the prophets' main subject matter, addressing the sin of the people. God raised up a prophet to take a stand and shout out loud that what was happening was not right. The covenant between the people and God was being broken by the people. And there were two major sins that were condemned over and over and over:

Idolatry
They were exchanging the worship of God for the worship of created things, worshipping the gods of other nations, and rejecting God. (Read Jeremiah 2:26-28.)
God had rescued them from slavery in Egypt, brought them to the land he had promised them, established them as a favored people, and they turned their backs on him!

Social Injustice

Their love for God was to be displayed in their actions toward others, but instead they had become a people who were only looking to their own self-interests. (Read Isaiah 58:3-10).

Over and over, God calls them out for idolatry and social injustice. Fast forward a few hundred years to Jesus' time. Do you remember when the teacher of the law asked him what the greatest commandment was? What did Jesus say was the greatest commandment? Love the Lord your God with all your heart and with all your soul and with all your mind. Then what did he say was the second? Love your neighbor as yourself. All the Law (the covenant in Leviticus/Deuteronomy) and the Prophets hang on these two commandments.

Can you see why God had lost patience with the people? You boil all the Old Testament instruction down to its simplest form and you get two commands: love God and love others. They were willfully disregarding both, and therefore all! Is it any wonder why God seems upset?

Remembering that God is doing the same thing today that he was doing back then, the next question is where are we at with these commands?

2. Judgment

If we had any doubt that God does not think our sin is funny, all we have to do is read through the prophets. If we had any thoughts that our attempts to justify our sin was fooling God, all we have to do is read through the prophets. If we have any question that God takes sin seriously, all we have to do is read through the prophets. (Read Amos 9:1-4)

God makes it very clear that continued rejection of him will bring about judgment. And it doesn't matter if it's "heathens" like Assyria or Edom, or if it's "God's people" like Israel and Judah.

Judgment is very real and a good reminder to us as we make decisions on how we are living. Throughout the scriptures, we see God to be a gracious and loving God, and we actually see that over and over in the prophets...but we must never forget that God hates sin.

3. Restoration

Throughout the books of the prophets, along with announcement of man's sin and pronouncement of God's judgment, is a concept that one day, restoration would come.

There is this idea that is spoken of called the Day of Yahweh, or the Day of the Lord, that would one day come. And it communicates this idea that when God comes to the earth, judgment comes with him, but so does restoration.

This concept is sometimes Israel-specific, speaking of a time when God's people would return from their exile in foreign lands. It is often also used to describe a day that will come in the future when God will restore all his original creation that was lost in the fall.

We talked in the last chapter about the theme of the entire Old Testament. It was God working to bring the entire world back to him by setting aside a group of people who would live under his rule as king. This was unique from the way the rest of the world lived. They would be a model for the world of the blessings of living in God's kingdom. This was true for Israel, and it's true for us as the church.

But God says, one day, the modeling will be done, and my rule over all the earth will be a complete reality. The day of the Lord will come, and with it, total restoration of what was lost. (Read Isaiah 65:17-25)

If I could impress upon you one thing about the message of the prophets, it would be this: Live as if the day of the Lord's coming is already here. We are to be today what the kingdom will be someday. We have been commissioned by God through his grace and the sacrifice of Jesus to be a part of his restoration process.

We are to live as if the day of the Lord's coming is already here!

Action Steps

- ❑ Read three chapters from a book of prophecy (Isaiah through Malachi).
- ❑ Read a commentary or more in-depth resource on one of the books of prophecy.
- ❑ Join a group that is studying the Bible (Growth Group, Men's or Women's ministry).
- ❑ Start a regular Bible reading plan.

Discussion Questions

1. Find the 17 prophets in your Old Testament. (The first 5 are called major because of their length.) Which of these do you know something about?

2. Share what you remember about each.

3. There were several messages that the prophets brought to the people of Israel (the northern kingdom) and Judah (the southern kingdom.) Look at each of the prophets listed below and find the ways that they address the main themes.

   Major Themes of OT Prophesy: Sin; Judgment; Restoration

   Hosea:

   Amos:

   Zephaniah:

   Haggai:

4. How do the prophesies of the OT apply to us today?

WISDOM LITERATURE

In this chapter we're focusing on the Books of Poetry, often called the Wisdom Literature, and I think that I would prefer that name instead, only because poetry often has negative connotations. We think artsy, flowery, romantic...boring!

They're called the Books of Poetry because they contain a good deal of content presented in a patterned style of writing. Most of the time, it wasn't necessarily rhyming like we think of poetry, but just a certain structure to their thoughts.

So if you hesitate when you hear the term poetry, don't give up on them just yet...

The Books of the Old Testament that are included as Poetry are Job, Psalms, Proverbs, Ecclesiastes, and Song of Songs.

The books of history focused on God's work with a people, with mankind, with a nation. These focus more on the individual and they are experiential rather than historical. Wisdom literature is called that because it's the *expression* of a person's life of faith.

We're going to look at each of the five books, and what we can learn to better understand them.

Job

Job is the oldest book in the Bible. It was written in the time of the patriarchs, about 2000 BC. Part of it is written like a narrative, and part is poetry.

Because it's so old, there's debate over whether Job was actually a historical person, or more of a parable, but it's generally thought that this was a story that people passed down through the generations by telling it over and over, maybe around the fire at night, or at gatherings.

Job is a man who was very wealthy and renowned among the people. He was blameless and upright. He feared God and shunned evil. The introduction describes how successful he was and how faithful he was to God.

Then the reader gets a peek behind the scenes, where Satan says that the only reason Job follows God is because God has protected and blessed him. So God allows Satan to take away everything Job has: children, wealth, health, and that will be a test to see if Job still follows God.

Job, of course, has no idea why this is happening. His friends come to comfort him and offer the traditional answer: God blesses those who do good and curses those who do evil. Therefore, Job must have sinned against God. Job, however, insists that he hasn't, and he doesn't understand why all these things are happening to him.

The book addresses one of the oldest questions of mankind: Why do bad things happen to good people? And you know what? The book of Job never really answers that question. The reader knows what's going on behind the scenes, because the narrator gives us information that Job doesn't know. But even though we know more about what's going on, we still don't learn why.

Here's one thing we learn from the poetic books, from the wisdom literature...they often raise questions but don't give us the answer. That's ok. It might drive some personality types nuts, but we learn that it's ok. Job is not meant to answer questions but show us an example of someone living a life of faith in spite of the questions.

Psalms

The book of Psalms is a collection of 150 writings, many from around the time of King David (~1000 BC), but others are later.

Psalm is a weird word to us, but it's from a Greek word, and the "P" is silent. One chapter of the book is a psalm (singular). The entire collection is called the book of Psalms (plural).

These psalms were songs, poems, and prayers of individuals expressing themselves and their feelings to God. They were collected together and often used as songs in religious events and on holidays, learned and known by the people of Israel.

It's as if the most emotional of indie rockers wrote song ideas in their journals, and they became anthems for an entire nation and people! It would be like singing Air Supply or Secondhand Serenade songs to start baseball games and wedding ceremonies.

Topics include praise to God, remembrance of things God has done for them, thanksgiving, songs of lament or anguish for pain and sin or situations they're in, and vindictive songs.

So here are some things we learn from the book of Psalms.

1. We can be completely transparent before God, and express to Him our emotions, whether we're thankful, depressed, impatient, content, angry, whatever. These people laid their souls bare before God.

2. As we read the Psalms we need to remember that these are expressions of emotion, and put that in the context of the big picture of the Bible. For example, just because someone cries out in Psalm 137 for God to destroy the babies of their enemy doesn't necessarily advocate that God desires that attitude from us.

3. Another thing to remember is that because these are artistic creative expressions, it can be dangerous to try to prove theological doctrines from the Psalms. This is poetry. What we can do is appreciate them as the experiences of those who have gone before us as they live in relationship with God and live out a life of faith.

Proverbs

Here we go, enough of the artsy stuff! This is the practical nitty-gritty how to live your best life stuff. Proverbs is a collection of sayings, of wise advice. Solomon is thought to be the collector (about 950 BC).

It is specifically directed at young men in an affluent society. If you read the first nine chapters it's fantastic advice for young people, especially guys.

But it's applicable to all, and the rest of the collection is life lessons. These are great, tried and true words of wisdom for all areas of life.

They are sayings that people probably quoted and remembered, just like we say "A stitch in time saves nine," or "don't count your chickens before they hatch."

Consider Proverbs 19:19-20. We read these and find helpful, wise advice for living a life of faith.

Guess what, though? Life is messy and confusing, and sometimes a wise saying won't solve the problem. Case in point: Proverbs 26:4-5 (sometimes contradictory).

What we learn is that proverbs are general principles about a life of faith, they are divinely observed patterns. But they're not promises or guarantees. Proverbs 22:6 (sometimes kids rebel).

The book of Job and the book of Proverbs kind of balance each other out. Proverbs says, there are general rules and principles that life usually follows, such as good things happen to good people, and bad things happen to bad people. Job says, yes but not always.

So we need to remember when we read the proverbs, they're generally true patterns, but not promises or guarantees.

Ecclesiastes

This book is traditionally attributed to Solomon, the third king of Israel, the son of David (about 950 BC). It is a collection of writings describing his search for the meaning in life.

The most famous section of Ecclesiastes is referenced in The Byrds' song, "To everything, turn, turn, turn, there is a season, turn, turn, turn." But there's a lot more to the book than that.

Ecclesiastes is one of the most depressing books in the Bible. I'm not sure what the Old Testament equivalent of Prozac was, but he wasn't taking it.

The theme of the book is "Meaningless! Meaningless! Everything is meaningless!"

The author recounts his efforts to find meaning and pleasure in life. He walks through wisdom/intellect/education, pleasures, work, advancement, and wealth. All of it, he concludes, falls short of giving meaning in life. Everything is meaningless!

Don't read this after a breakup or you get fired. It will only make you more depressed. Actually, maybe it's a great book to read, because it will remind you that those things aren't worth basing your life on.

After working to find meaning in all of these things, the book concludes with this: Ecclesiastes 12:13-14.

The conclusion is to enjoy life, but do so in keeping with God's commandments, because we'll have to account for the things we do.

Again...good words of advice in poetic form...this is the wisdom literature, or books of poetry.

Song of Songs (or Song of Solomon)

This book was also traditionally authored by Solomon (about 950 BC).

If these books were at Barnes & Noble, Job would be a biography of a distinguished looking man, with the title "Faithful through Trial." Song of Songs is a Harlequin romance novel. Leviticus is probably the least-read book of the Bible. Song of Songs is probably the least admitted-to-being-read book of the Bible.

It is a play or story with two main characters, a Lover and his Beloved. It outlines the interaction of their courtship and their expressions of love for each other.

This is not Disney Channel type romantic language, either. Some of this is junior high locker room humor. This is not typically a part of the Bible we typically preach from on Sunday mornings.

Historically, there have been three approaches to interpreting Song of Songs.

One is that it is a drama written by Solomon. Another is that it is a collection of love poems. A third is that it is a metaphor, because some are uncomfortable with the language and subject matter, it's interpreted as God and Israel, or Christ and his church.

I personally hold the first view, it makes the most sense, and I actually get a little creeped out about the third view.

Again, the book is a creative expression of emotion, it highlights the pleasures of emotional and physical love for another person.

Remember, the big picture of the Old Testament helps us understand how to read the specific books.

Our job is to read it like the people of old did, within the framework and lens of people living according to God's covenant.

Application

What do we learn from the books of Poetry?

As we read, **we need to understand the style of literature as we're interpreting what it means and what God might be trying to teach us.** Remember the characteristics of wisdom literature…creative expressions of people living out their experiences as followers of God.

We need to value creative expressions of faith experiences today. Somehow when we become adults, we think that being creative is only for a select few. Where did that come from? Every one of us when we were younger busted a move to Elvis, or Michael Jackson, or N*Sync. Why do we now think that only special people can express themselves in creative ways? If God, who is a creator, made us in his image, we all have the ability to create, whether through the arts, or with our hands, or with our heads. So the question is, what creative expression are you producing to give honor and glory to God?

These days we're so often consumed with accomplishing tasks or being productive that we don't often give ourselves time and breathing room just to be creative. As the people of God, this would be a valuable practice! What creative expression are you producing to give honor and glory to God?

Action Steps

- ☐ Read three chapters from a book of poetry (Job through Song of Songs).
- ☐ Read a commentary or more in-depth resource on one of the books of poetry.
- ☐ Join a group that is studying the Bible (Growth Group, Men's or Women's ministry).
- ☐ Start a regular Bible reading plan.

Discussion Questions

1. Look at each of the following passages and then share which is your favorite and why.
   - Job 38
   - Psalms 23
   - Proverbs 31:10-31
   - Ecclesiastes 3:1-8
   - Song of Solomon 1:1-4

2. Consider Job. He lost everything and refused to curse God. Eventually he questioned God and then God responded with a testimony to his power and supremacy. Read Job's final word to God in Job 42:2-6.

3. Recall or look through Psalms and Proverbs. Are there any passages which have special meaning for you?

4. Have you ever read through Ecclesiastes? Song of Solomon? Did you know that Solomon was the richest man in the world, built the most magnificent Temple ever on earth, had 300 wives, and 700 concubines? How does this play into Ecclesiastes and Song of Solomon?

BIOGRAPHY

The Good News

25 Now there are also many other things that Jesus did. Were every one of them to be written, I suppose that the world itself could not contain the books that would be written.

John 21:25

When I was in High School in Escanaba (many years ago) I encouraged a friend of mine to read the New Testament. It only took her a couple of days to read Matthew, Mark, Luke, and John. After she had completed them she was confused, asked, "Why do they tell the same stories?"

When you read the gospels you discover that none of them deliver a full account of the life of Jesus and that they seem to repeat the same stories. Yet, there are great gaps in His life which none of the authors cover.

After the record of His birth and infant years nothing whatever is told us about Him until He had reached the age of twelve and then we only get one brief glimpse of when He was a boy visiting the Temple at Jerusalem with Mary and Joseph.

Nothing further is told us about Him until He had reached the age of thirty.

Even when we come to the accounts of His public ministry, the records are fragmentary. The authors select only portions of His teachings and describe in detail just a few of His miracles.

So what is going on here? Why are these books written and presented the way that they are? Why are some stories repeated from one to another and why are others left out or told from a different angle?

The four Gospels (The Story of Good News) are each complete in itself and each of which is written with a distinctive design.

Most people don't realize that each of the four authors was writing a complete work to a specific group. Each of these individual books (called a gospel which means "good news") was written according to a design and plan. Nothing was brought into any one of these writings unless it was relevant to the overall theme and audience that the book is written to address.

Consider Teddy Roosevelt and the idea of four different men writing four separate biographies – each with a particular view of the man.

- The Sportsman
- The Military Leader
- The President
- The Husband and Father

For instance: suppose it was known that Mr. Roosevelt, as a boy, had excelled in gymnastics and athletics which of his biographers would mention this fact? Clearly, the one who was depicting him as a sportsman would mention it.

Suppose that as a boy Mr. Roosevelt had frequently engaged in fist fights, which one would make mention of it? Evidently, the one who was depicting his military career, for it would serve to illustrate his fighting qualities.

Again, suppose that when a college-student Mr. Roosevelt had displayed an aptitude for debating, which biographer would refer to it? The fourth, which was telling about his political and presidential life, would record this part of the story.

Finally, suppose that from youth upwards Mr. Roosevelt had shown that he loved kids. Which of his biographers would refer to it? The last, for he is telling about the ex-president's private and domestic life.[1]

Each of these authors has a particular view because of their background and a specific audience because of their place in life. Let's look at each.

Matthew

Matthew speaks of Jesus as the Christ, the son of David, and king of the Jews. Matthew presents Christ in Kingdom connections, as the One who possessed the title to reign over Israel. How fitting, then, that Matthew, an officer of a vast empire, should be the one selected for this task.

Like all Jews, Matthew longed for the coming of the kingdom of God. Someday there would be a great king and who would bring a new era of strength and power to the world and it would be through David – the great king of Israel! That meant a lot to Matthew.

Matthew was a publican – a tax collector. The Romans appointed locals to collect the taxes from their peers. Because they were seen as collaborators (which they were!) they were hated by the Jews more bitterly than the Romans themselves.

As one who was socially rejected he wrote with great feeling of the one who was "hated without a cause" and talked about the Messiah-Savior, as "despised and rejected" by His own people.

Also, in God appointing this man, who was connected with the Romans, we also anticipate the grace of God reaching out to the despised Gentiles.

Imagine that if you went to Jerusalem today there is a good chance you would meet a man who I'll call "Ravid." Ravid is a Jew. Not a particularly religious man he is still very much a Jewish man. The traditions of Judaism are strong. He knows of God and the teachings of Judaism concerning the many

[1]Arthur Walkington Pink, *Why Four Gospels?* (Oak Harbor, WA: Logos Research Systems, Inc., 1999).

43

prophesies about how God was going to someday make all wrongs right.

Now picture Matthew sitting down and talking to this man. Consider what he includes in his account of the life of Jesus.

Matthew begins with Jesus' Lineage.

The book of the genealogy of Jesus Christ, the son of David, the son of Abraham. Abraham was the father of Isaac...and Jacob the father of Joseph the husband of Mary, of whom Jesus was born, who is called Christ.

Matthew 1:1, 2, &16

He showed him the genealogies that proved Jesus was of the line of David – physically through Mary and legally through Joseph. Matthew began to show him that Jesus was that man!

Everything in his narrative centers on this truth. This explains why the first Gospel opens with a setting forth of Christ's royal genealogy.

Matthew tells of the Wise Men who worshiped the new King.

Now after Jesus was born in Bethlehem of Judea in the days of Herod the king, behold, wise men from the east came to Jerusalem, saying, "Where is he who has been born king of the Jews? For we saw his star when it rose and have come to worship him."

Matthew 2:1-2

It is important to Matthew that the reader understands why the wise men from the East, who came to Jerusalem inquiring "Where is He that is born King of the Jews?".

Throughout his writing Matthew tells what Jesus said about the coming Kingdom.

"The kingdom of heaven is like treasure hidden in a field, which a man found and covered up. Then in his joy he goes and sells all that he has and buys that field.

Matthew 13:44

Matthew records that Pilate called him the "King of the Jews."

And over his head they put the charge against him, which read, "This is Jesus, the King of the Jews."

Matthew 27:37

Clearly Matthew's singular theme was that Jesus was the king who had come to establish David's throne in the new Kingdom of Heaven.

His writing is all about how the Old Testament prophesies are fulfilled in and through Jesus – King of the Jews – the Messiah who the prophets of old had promised would someday come.

Mark

Mark had a completely different take on Jesus. Mark speaks of Jesus as the mighty worker of God's will.

…Get Mark and bring him with you, for he is very useful to me for ministry.

2 Timothy 4:11b

This is John Mark who ran from Garden of Gethsemane – naked. His story is recorded only in the gospel of Mark – which is why scholars believe it was the author. Who else would know and who else would bother to mention it?

He is also the man who went on the first Missionary Journey with Paul and Barnabas and then bailed out early. He was a good friend of Peter's and my guess is that they were probably a lot alike.

Imagine that Mark had a young activist friend named Jules. He would be like one of those people who traveled to NYC and lived in the park during "Occupy Wall Street". He wasn't interested in promises and process. He wanted action. He wanted to do something to change the world and nothing he did made any difference but he kept hearing stories about a man named Jesus.

Mark told him about this revolutionary man of peace that rocked the world.

He told about the One who though equal with God made Himself of no reputation and "took upon Him the form of a servant."

Everything in this second Gospel contributes to this central theme, and everything foreign to it is rigidly excluded.

This explains why there is no genealogy recorded in Mark, why Christ is introduced at the beginning of His public ministry (nothing whatever being told us here of His earlier life), and why there are more miracles (deeds of service) detailed here than in any of the other Gospels.[2]

Mark records Jesus as a man of action.

- Jesus is baptized by John.
- Jesus is tempted in the wilderness.
- Jesus begins His ministry.
- Jesus calls His first disciples.
- Jesus heals a man with an unclean spirit.
- Jesus heals Peter's mother-in-law and many others.
- Jesus preaches and casts out demons.
- Jesus cleanses a Leper.

Mark writes of all these things Jesus did... in the first chapter! Mark is a man of action and Jesus is presented to those in the Roman Empire that value accomplishment.

Mark tells of the revolutionary Servant who came to change the world.

- He enters Jerusalem on a colt.
- He accepts the praise of the crowds.
- He curses the fig tree.
- He cleanses the Temple.
- He confounds the chief priests, scribes, and elders.

---

[2] Arthur Walkington Pink, *Why Four Gospels?* (Oak Harbor, WA: Logos Research Systems, Inc., 1999).

Jesus was not about the status quo. He rocked the boat and shook up the establishment. Jesus was all about hope and change – to coin a phrase we've heard a lot in the last few years.

Luke

Luke had a totally different agenda than either Matthew who wrote to the Jewish and ruling elite or Mark who wrote to the revolutionary, the activist, and the conqueror. Luke was the careful historian. Listen to how he begins his writing.

In Luke Jesus is proclaimed to be the Son of Man.

Inasmuch as many have undertaken to compile a narrative of the things that have been accomplished among us, just as those who from the beginning were eyewitnesses and ministers of the word have delivered them to us, it seemed good to me also, having followed all things closely for some time past, to write an orderly account for you, most excellent Theophilus, that you may have certainty concerning the things you have been taught.

Luke 1:1-4

Luke is the careful historian who writes to the dedicated learner. He writes to a specific person named Theophilus.

Theophilus, literally, means lover of God. It may be a real person or it may be a virtual representation of all those who are interested in knowing God.

Luke was a physician, a friend and companion of Paul.

His writings came later than the first two and were compiled with notes from all over.

Imagine that Luke had a friend named Ted who was a professor of history and literature. He loved to examine the lessons of time and culture and was well traveled. He wrote many articles and was a tenured professor at Harvard.

Luke sat down with Ted one afternoon and told him all about Jesus.

Luke traces Jesus beginning back to Adam.

Jesus, when he began his ministry, was about thirty years of age, being the son (as was supposed) of Joseph, the son of Heli…the son of Enos, the son of Seth, the son of Adam, the son of God.

Luke 3:23-38

Everything in the narrative serves to bring this out. This explains why the third Gospel traces His genealogy back to Adam, the first man, (instead of to Abraham only, as in Matthew), why as the perfect Man He is seen here so frequently in prayer, and why the angels are seen ministering to Him, instead of commanded by Him as they are in Matthew.[3]

Luke's Gospel deals with our Lord's Humanity, and presents Him as "The" Son of Man who is related to but contrasted with the sons of men.

Luke's Gospel gives us the fullest account of the virgin-birth.

Luke's Gospel also reveals more fully than any of the others the fallen and depraved state of human nature. He tells us why we needed God to come in the flesh to be one of us.

He also writes with an international pen. Unlike Matthew he deals with more than the Jewish heritage. He speaks of Jesus reaching out to all people.

Luke Reaches out to the Gentile.

And then they will see the Son of Man coming in a cloud with power and great glory. Now when these things begin to take place, straighten up and raise your heads, because your redemption is drawing near."

Luke 21:27-28

Again; Luke's Gospel is far more international in its scope than the other three, and is more Gentilish than Jewish.

Remember that Luke was a physician. He was a student of human nature and cared for all no matter where they came from.

Moreover, there is good reason to believe that Luke himself was not a Jew but a Gentile, and hence it was peculiarly fitting

---

[3]Arthur Walkington Pink, *Why Four Gospels?*(Oak Harbor, WA: Logos Research Systems, Inc., 1999).

that he should present Christ not as "the Son of David" but as "The Son of Man."[4]

The Synoptic Gospels

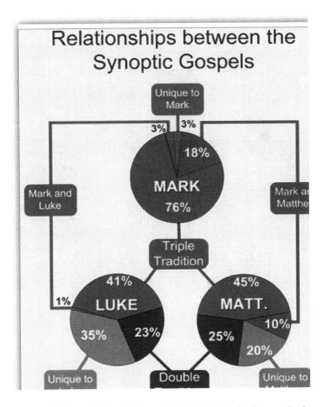

These first three Gospels are called by scholars the "synoptic" gospels. Even though they recorded the life and ministry of Jesus differently than one another according to their purpose and their audience – they told much the same story with many of the same events.

---

[4]Arthur Walkington Pink, *Why Four Gospels?*(Oak Harbor, WA: Logos Research Systems, Inc., 1999).

John

John was completely different. John wrote a book that was different than that which was written by all of the first three authors.

John reveals Jesus to be the Son of God.

In the beginning was the Word, and the Word was with God, and the Word was God... And the Word became flesh and dwelt among us, and we have seen his glory, glory as of the only Son from the Father, full of grace and truth.

John 1:1 & 14

John is one of the sons of thunder. He is also known as a man of compassion in the inner circle (Peter, James, and John.) He is called the apostle of Love and he sat on one side of Jesus in the upper room. Judas Iscariot was on the other side so John saw his compassion and his pain – up close and personal. John was the only apostle at the cross of Jesus.

Imagine that John had a friend named Patrick. Patrick was a philosopher and a counselor who was deeply concerned about the wounds in a person's soul.

He is passionate about helping people be whole and to experience true happiness – to find real joy filled life.

Everything in this fourth Gospel is made to illustrate and demonstrate this Divine relationship. This explains why in the opening verse we are carried back to a point before time began, and we are shown Christ as the Word "in the beginning," with God, and Himself expressly declared to be God.

John gives many of Jesus divine titles.

The next day he saw Jesus coming toward him, and said, "Behold, the <u>Lamb of God</u>, who takes away the sin of the world!

John 1:29

"For God so loved the world, that he gave <u>his only Son</u>, that whoever believes in him should not perish but have eternal life.

John 3:16

The woman said to him, "I know that <u>Messiah</u> is coming (he who is called <u>Christ</u>). When he comes, he will tell us all things." Jesus said to her, "I who speak to you am he."

John 4:25-26

John gives us many of His divine titles, like "The only begotten of the Father," the "Lamb of God," the "Light of the world", etc. It is John who tells us that prayer should be made in His Name, and why the Holy Spirit is here said to be sent from the Son as well as from the Father.

John reveals Jesus is God.

This was why the Jews were seeking all the more to kill him, because not only was he breaking the Sabbath, but he was even calling God his own Father, making himself equal with God.

John 5:18

Jesus said to them, "Truly, truly, I say to you, before Abraham was, I am." So they picked up stones to throw at him, but Jesus hid himself and went out of the temple.

John 8:58-59

John's Gospel presents Christ in the loftiest character of all, setting Him forth in Divine relationship, showing that He was the Son of God. This was a task that called for a man of high spirituality, one who was intimate with our Lord in a special manner, one who was gifted with unusual spiritual discernment. And John, "the disciple whom Jesus loved," was nearer to the Savior than any of the twelve. He was well chosen.

How fitting that the one who leaned on the Master should be the instrument to portray Christ as "The only-begotten Son of God. Thus may we discern and admire the manifold wisdom of God in equipping the four "Evangelists" for their honorous work.[5]

Which Gospel is for you?

The Good News is only good news when it's personal and real. Each is written with an audience in mind. One of the four will be more meaningful to you than the others but each has something to say.

- Matthew – Jesus came to build a new Kingdom
- Mark – Jesus came to change the world
- Luke – Jesus came for the whole world
- John – Jesus came for me!

[5]Arthur Walkington Pink, *Why Four Gospels?*(Oak Harbor, WA: Logos Research Systems, Inc., 1999).

Action Steps

- ☐ Become a disciple of Jesus
- ☐ Read one of the four Gospels this week
- ☐ Pray for _____ every day this week.
- ☐ Pray an opportunity to tell someone why you follow Jesus

Discussion Questions

1. Each of the Gospels had a different theme and audience. Which is the most meaningful to you personally? Why?
   - Matthew – Jesus came to build a new Kingdom
   - Mark – Jesus came to change the world
   - Luke – Jesus came for the whole world
   - John – Jesus is the loving God

2. Take a quick look at Matthew. How do you see the "Jewish" flavor coming through? Who in our world would benefit from reading Matthew?

3. Take a look through Mark. How do see the revolutionary and suffering servant revealed? Who do you know that would learn about Jesus best from Mark's writing?

4. Skim through Luke. Do you see Luke's background as a physician and Gentile in the text? What kind of people today would learn best from Luke?

5. Skim through John Quickly. How is it different than the other gospels? Who would learn the best from John?

Rick Stacy

NT HISTORY

The Acts of the Apostles

Simon Peter replied, "You are the Christ, the Son of the living God...
18 And I tell you, you are Peter, and on this rock I will build my church,
and the gates of hell shall not prevail against it.

Matthew 16:16 & 18

Jesus gave up the glory of heaven to come to our world for one purpose... to build his eternal kingdom which will be filled with his people. Today, he is gathering those people who walk by faith and follow him into his church.

The book of acts is the record of the beginning of this great work. It was written by Luke, the same man who wrote the gospel. Like the gospel of Luke, this writing is also addressed to Theophilus whose name means "lover of God."

While this book stands on its own it is written as part of an ongoing story of Jesus establishing his kingdom – through his body, the church.

We call the book the "Acts of the Apostles" but a more accurate title would be the "Acts of God." This is the narrative of how God worked through a few men who were called by Jesus to establish his Kingdom on earth.

In fact there are over 120 mentions of God in first 13 chapters of Acts. This is all about what happens when God empowers his people.

It's inspiring and awesome to see the Kingdom of God – the church – become a tsunami that washed across Jerusalem, Judea, Samaria, Asia, and Europe in a matter of a few years.

Acts is a key and critically important document to Christians. It outlines not only the beginning of the church but it also documents some essential teachings and practices that define the church… to this very day. The book of Acts is the record of the establishment of God's Kingdom on earth.

Jesus had made it clear that he had come to save the souls of men and to build his church. Now he continues his work through the Church.

But you will receive power when the Holy Spirit has come upon you, and you will be my witnesses in Jerusalem and in all Judea and Samaria, and to the end of the earth."

Acts 1:8

Jerusalem – Pentecost

When the day of Pentecost arrived, they were all together in one place. And suddenly there came from heaven a sound like a mighty rushing wind, and it filled the entire house where they were sitting.

Acts 2:1-2

In the first chapter the disciples and the Apostles wait on God. In the second chapter of Acts God makes his move and the Holy Spirit fills the Apostles with power. There is the sound of a strong wind – but nothing moves. Lightning shoots down from the sky and on each of the heads of the apostles there are flames. These guys are literally on fire for God! Then the real action starts. They begin to speak about Jesus and the people listening understand what they are saying – in their own language.

The word spreads fast and the people come from all over the city and stand in the streets below the building where the apostles are gathered. Then Peter begins to speak.

He tells them about Jesus and about their part of the crucifixion of God's son. He tells them that this is the day that the world changes forever and he quotes Joel 2:28.

The Day the World Changed!

"And it shall come to pass afterward, that I will pour out my Spirit on all flesh; your sons and your daughters shall prophesy, your old men shall dream dreams, and your young men shall see visions.

Even on the male and female servants in those days I will pour out my Spirit.

"And I will show wonders in the heavens and on the earth, blood and fire and columns of smoke. The sun shall be turned to darkness, and the moon to blood, before the great and awesome day of the Lord comes.

And it shall come to pass that everyone who calls on the name of the Lord shall be saved. For in Mount Zion and in Jerusalem there shall be those who escape, as the Lord has said, and among the survivors shall be those whom the Lord calls.

Joel 2:28-32

Jesus has torn down the dark shroud of death. The heavy black weight of sin has been removed and the gateway to heaven has now been opened.

Our God is a God of life! He has conquered the grave and sent Satan a final message that he has lost the battle, the war and his grip on the soul of every man, woman, youth, or child that turns his heart to Jesus.

Jesus has called for us all!

When they heard the word of Peter they were convicted of their sin and in faith turned their hearts to Jesus. 3000 were baptized into Jesus that first amazing day!

The next few chapters describe the church growing with exuberance, power, and strength. It spreads across the city like an unstoppable tsunami gathering up the lost, the hopeless, and the hurting into the assembly of the saved – the church – the Kingdom of God. This was the beginning of the church… the kingdom of God on earth.

But eventually there are two challenges.

First, there was a murmuring among the people because some of the Grecian Jewish widows were being overlooked in the daily distribution of food. The Apostles had the people appoint deacons or ministering servants (that's what the word deacon means) to oversee the needs and organize the efforts of the church ministry.

There was a second and more pressing problem, the opposition that came from the Jewish leaders. This came mostly from a sect of teachers called Pharisees. They had been the primary religious leaders of the Jewish community for decades and weren't about to step aside quietly. They got the Apostles arrested and demanded that they stop talking about Jesus. When the Apostles would not be intimidated or quieted the Pharisees started pressing harder. In chapter seven one of the deacons, Stephen, was arrested, charged with blasphemy, and killed by stoning. This began the second phase of expansion.

Strangely, it was fueled by persecution.

Judea & Samaria – Persecution

"…And there arose on that day a great persecution against the church in Jerusalem, and they were all scattered throughout the regions of Judea and Samaria, except the apostles."

Acts 8:1

When Stephen was killed his life, his speech, and his death became a powerful testimony in Jerusalem and in all of Judea and Samaria.

The pressure brought on the believers by the Pharisees acted like water being thrown on a grease fire. It didn't put it out. No, it exploded with even greater power in every direction of the compass and throughout the surrounding territories. Everywhere the people went they told and retold the story of Jesus and of Stephen.

A revival broke out in Samaria and the Apostles sent Peter and others to find out what was happening and to tell even more people about the way of God through Jesus.

One of the evangelists, by the name of Phillip, was diverted from the work of the revival in Samaria to an empty road between Jerusalem and Gaza where he met a man who was the treasurer of the Queen of Ethiopia. This man became a believer and was baptized and so the church began its spread to Egypt and Africa.

Then... another marvelous step. Salvation came to the Gentiles. First, Peter had an encounter with a man named Cornelius, a non-Jew who wanted to follow Jesus. Peter wasn't certain about what to do until God made it clear through a vision that Jesus came for all men – not just some. Peter baptized Cornelius and the church began to expand further into the world of Gentiles

This last step was led, not by Peter who opened the doorway, but by another man. Saul who had stood by when Stephen was killed and became a believer. His name was changed to Paul and he took the good news of Jesus to the ends of the earth.

The Ends of the Earth – Paul, Apostle to the Gentiles

While they were worshiping the Lord and fasting, the Holy Spirit said, "Set apart for me Barnabas and Saul for the work to which I have called them." Then after fasting and praying they laid their hands on them and sent them off.

Acts 13:2-3

Paul was called by Jesus directly in a vision on the road to Damascus. He was going there to kill and imprison these pesky Christians. His purpose was to stamp out this blasphemous cult. But on that road the powerful light of Jesus penetrated his heart and Saul became Paul, the Apostle to the Gentile nations.

Three times in the last half of the book Paul tells his story of conversion and transformation on the road to Damascus. Three times Paul travels to tell the Gentiles about Jesus.

The first missionary trip was to Sicily and then Asia. It was very successful but forced a confrontation between the party of the circumcised and the Gentiles. A meeting between all the Apostles, and leaders of the church in Jerusalem was called and the question of Gentile salvation was carefully considered. It was resolved with joy and ambition to continue to grow the church.

So Paul and Silas went back to Asia and then to Greece and the rest of Europe in two more mission trips. Churches were established in every city – first in the synagogues and then among the Gentiles.

The whole of the Roman Empire began to take notice. The opposition got stronger and Paul was arrested while reporting to the church on his last mission trip. He was charged with blasphemy and sedition against the Roman Government.

He appealed to Caesar and began his final journey to Rome. In Rome he was chained to the Praetorian Guard and held under house arrest. In these circumstances for two years (about 63-64 AD) where he was able to reach and teach everyone who came to him – and many came. On top of that many of the Praetorian Guard became believers. When they retired after their years of service they were commonly appointed as ambassadors to the far flung corners of the empire... and so the church continued to grow.

Acts closes with Paul waiting for his hearing before Caesar. Tacitus tells us that Nero burned Rome in 64 AD and blamed the Christians. Paul was beheaded at about this time in history.

Besides the story of the expansion of the growth of the church there are some key themes in the book of Acts.

Key Themes in Acts

These themes are important because they define the nature and character of the church – then and now.

God's Salvation

Now when they heard this they were cut to the heart, and said to Peter and the rest of the apostles, "Brothers, what shall we do?" And Peter said to them, "Repent and be baptized every one of you in the name of Jesus Christ for the forgiveness of your sins, and you will receive the gift of the Holy Spirit.
Acts 2:37-38

In the first message of salvation delivered by Peter on the day of Pentecost he laid out the elements that are essential to our understanding of what Jesus did on the cross and how we are called to respond.

Peter teaches about the important element related to salvation.
- Sin & Judgment (Rebellion against God)
- Crucifixion and Redemption
- Faith and Repentance
- Baptism and the Gift of the Holy Spirit

In baptism we come in contact with both God's mercy (forgiveness) and his grace (life)

This teaching is played out over and over in the book of Acts. We see one example after another. Consider the 3000 on the day of Pentecost; the Ethiopian; the Philippian Jailor; and even Saul who became Paul.

Christian Practices

And they devoted themselves to the apostles' teaching and the fellowship, to the breaking of bread and the prayers.
Acts 2:42

Here we see the church acting every day the practices of the church – which make it different than every other group in the history of humanity. The people of the way (as it was called in the early days of the church) were devoted to four practices.

Apostles Teaching – In Acts 17:10-11 the people in Berea were held up in honor because they searched the OT scriptures to see if the things the Apostles were saying were true. We also should be a people of the word of God.

Fellowship of Believers – Acts 2:42 the church is described as a spiritual family that takes care of one another and makes sure that the needs – spiritual, physical, and emotional are being met by the others in the body of Christ.

Lord's Supper - Acts 20:7 tells us that the early church made it their practice to meet every Sunday in honor of Jesus' resurrection to break bread (take communion) and to worship their Lord. What a great habit and practice to have in our lives today!

Prayer – Acts 6:4 tells us that the Apostles appointed deacons to administrate the resources of the body to meet the needs of the church so that they could focus on the ministry of the word of God and prayer. Prayer is an important practice of the church – then and now.

There were two more key themes that helped to shape the church. One we have already talked about and that Jesus didn't die for the Jewish people only but also for the Gentile nations.

Gentile Redemption

If then God gave the same gift to them as he gave to us when we believed in the Lord Jesus Christ, who was I that I could stand in God's way?" When they heard these things they fell silent. And they glorified God, saying, "Then to the Gentiles also God has granted repentance that leads to life."
Acts 11:17-18

Peter witnessed that the same power of God that fell on him and the other Apostles on the day of Pentecost also came on

Cornelius and his house. The conclusion was inescapable. Jesus calls all who would put their faith in him to salvation!

That was settled early in chapter 10 and 11 of Acts but the details were worked out in chapter 15 at the council in Jerusalem after the first missionary journey of Paul and Barnabas.

Jesus vs. the Law

For it has seemed good to the Holy Spirit and to us to lay on you no greater burden than these requirements: that you abstain from what has been sacrificed to idols, and from blood, and from what has been strangled, and from sexual immorality. If you keep yourselves from these, you will do well..."

Acts 15:28-29

The question was really quite simple. Did Gentiles need to become Jewish converts as well as Jesus converts to be saved? In other words, did Cornelius and others like him need to be circumcised and to follow the whole of Mosaic law, keeping the Sabbath and celebrating the feasts or were they only to follow Jesus.

The council of Jerusalem agreed that the Law of Moses was replaced and overridden by word of our Lord Jesus. The clear message from God was that we are not under the law. We follow Jesus – he is our law. (In the next chapter we'll look at that in the letters in great detail.)

The decision was made to send an encouraging admonition (Acts 15:28-29) to all the gentile believers – which Paul happily did.

The Church prevails

Simon Peter replied, "You are the Christ, the Son of the living God... And I tell you, you are Peter, and on this rock I will build my church, and the gates of hell shall not prevail against it.

Matthew 16:16 & 18

Some years ago I read an article written by a man raised in a sect of believers that taught that the Mosaic law was still in effect. When he was confronted with the teachings of Paul about the freedom from the Law we have in Jesus it rocked his world.

He said, "You've taken away all the things I hold onto, all the festivals, all the Sabbath days, all the religious rules, now all I have is Jesus!"

I submit to you that Jesus is all we need! When we have Jesus the church prevails

I know we win because I looked at the end of the book.

Action Steps

- ❑ Do you believe? Repent and be baptized
- ❑ Read a chapter a day in Acts
- ❑ Do something for another believer
- ❑ Commit to come to worship every Sunday possible
- ❑ Pray for the church and leaders

Discussion Questions

1. Acts 2 describes a powerful beginning of the church. Have you ever felt the Spirit of God move with power in and through his church? What did you experience?

2. In Acts 8 the church endured the first of many persecutions and the church spread and grew. Have you ever endured criticism, rejection, or persecution for your faith in Jesus? If our church was openly persecuted today how would it change us?

3. Paul had a dramatic conversion experience. If you are a believer what was your conversion experience? Dramatic and public or quiet and personal?

4. Why was the Jerusalem council in Acts 15 so important? How does it affect the work of the church today in our community?

5. What does God want you to do today?

Rick Stacy

LETTERS

Love Letters[6]

Mortimer Adler, who was once the editor of the *Encyclopedia Britannica* wrote a best-seller titled *How to Read a Book*. In his book he said there is only one time that people really read what is written – when it's a love letter. Here is what he said.

There is only one situation that I can think of in which men and women make an effort to read better than they usually do. When they are in love and are reading a love letter, they read for all they are worth.

Mortimer Adler

Adler goes on to say, "They read every word three ways; they read between the lines and in the margins; they read the whole in terms of the parts, and each part in terms of the whole; they grow sensitive to context and ambiguity, to insinuation and implication; they perceive the color of words, the odor of phrases, and the weight of sentences"[7]

---

[6] Much of this message was taken, edited and rewritten using an article by Matt Procter in The Christian Standard as the foundation for the teaching.
http://christianstandard.com/2011/10/getting-the-most-from-the-epistles-part-one/

You should think of the epistles in the New Testament as love letters. If you do it will help you to read them for everything they can tell you about God. Read them as if you are a young person on their first journey away from home. Read them as if you have crossed the ocean and your father is half a world away and then after months on your own you get a letter.

This is what is really amazing about the Bible. God did not only include the historical narratives, the stories, and the formation of his law. Not only did he see to it that we have a record of the prophetic voices and the poetry of the past. He has also sent us letters. In fact, I don't know of one other sacred book in the entire world that is composed of letters.

Up until the last few years letters were the most personal form of communication available to anyone. In the early days of the church it was the only method of personal communication with the exception of sitting down and talking with someone at dinner. To have a letter from God was an amazing idea to people who were used to the gods being in their own worlds and who played with humanity. The idea of God wanting a personal relationship is astonishing and nothing short of mind blowing.

Except for the presence of God in the flesh in the person of Jesus a letter from God is as personal as it gets.

So think of these epistles as love letters. They are heartfelt words from a groom to his bride. We had better read for all we are worth. Take the time to read them carefully and reflect on what God is saying to you personally in these letters.

---

[7]Cited in Mortimer Adler, *How to Speak, How to Listen.*

Read and Reflect

Think over what I say, for the Lord will give you understanding in everything.

2 Timothy 2:7

The Epistles have more significant thoughts per square inch than other types of biblical literature. Compared to secular literature, well, there is no real comparison.

Sometimes that leads people to throw up their hands and to say that only scholars can understand it so why should I even try?

Let me take a moment to offer some encouragement.

In 2 Timothy 2:7, Paul tells Timothy, "Think over what I say, for the Lord will give you understanding in everything." When you ask God to help you and you spend some time thinking about his word to you – then knowledge, understanding, and even wisdom comes.

So relax, dig in, and enjoy exploring all the understanding for life that God offers you in his letters to you.

Before you dive in it would be helpful to understand some key ideas about what exactly a New Testament Epistle is.

The Epistle were letters

There are more epistles in the New Testament than any other kinds of writing. There are a total of 21 books out of 27.

So what is an epistle? (One little girl thought an *epistle* was "the wife of an apostle"!)

An *epistle* was a letter in the ancient world designed for wide circulation that addressed current issues and was based on a personal relationship.

Epistles follow a simple format:

Prescript

Here the writer identifies himself and his recipients (which seems a smarter approach than our modern letter template which doesn't reveal the writer's name until the letter's closing).

Greetings

Here the writer often expresses a prayer for the recipient's good health.

Body

Here the writer conveys his primary message—which may be personal, business, or official in nature.

Exhortations

Here the writer gives final instructions based upon the message he has already shared.

Closing

Here the writer passes along other greetings and a final salutation or prayer.

The New Testament writers adapted this basic format by "Christianizing" it. For example, instead of "hello" and "hope you're having a good day," they began with greetings like "grace and peace."

They also wrote much longer letters than secular letters from the time. (They were preachers, after all.) Cicero's average letter was 295 words, Seneca's was 955 words, but Paul's letters averaged 2,500 words!

The Epistles were Sermons

In fact, it is helpful to think of the Epistles as published sermons.

As a preacher for over 40 years, this is an especially meaningful to me. I have a wide variety of tools that can be used in a sermon.

To explain a point, I can choose from many different options to teach what the scripture means. I can tell a story, share a comparison, a statistic, a definition, a quotation, a joke, or a poem. And now days I can even put a video up on the screen.

A significant feature of the letters in the New Testament is that they too use many different options to illustrate and teach. As a reader of the New Testament letters, it will be helpful for you to understand something about a few of these tools:

Hymns

To the King of the ages, immortal, invisible, the only God, be honor and glory forever and ever. Amen.

1 Timothy 1:17

Paul often quotes ancient Christian hymns, and at other times, in places like 1 Timothy 1:17, he interrupts himself by bursting into a song of praise.

I knew of a preacher who did this (not me!) and would in the middle of a message break into a beautiful song of worship. It was an incredibly effective way of imprinting the message on the hearts of the people.

Hymns are a powerful way of teaching God's truth. Songs have been used for as long as there have been families and campfires to tell stories to the listeners.

Household Rules

Bondservants are to be submissive to their own masters in everything; they are to be well-pleasing, not argumentative, not pilfering, but showing all good faith, so that in everything they may adorn the doctrine of God our Savior.

Titus 2:9-10

Ancient teachers, like Aristotle, sometimes drew up a "household code" or a collection of advice to the head of a

Greco-Roman household on how to rule his wife, children, and slaves to ensure an ordered society.

Letters like the one to Titus often included a similar "household code" pattern – with some important differences.

First, God's codes included guidance for all the household members. Aristotle's code laid out the rules only for the household's "inferior" members (wives, children, slaves).

Second, all the members of the household were treated as equals before God. In the Greek and Roman codes the "inferior" members were often treated as property with no rights.

Third, the purpose behind the biblical codes was not to protect the social order, but to advance the gospel and the church.

Look at the last phrase in what Paul wrote here to Titus.

A third way of writing seen in these letters is lists of vices and virtues.

Vice and Virtue Lists

Now the works of the flesh are evident: sexual immorality, impurity, sensuality…

But the fruit of the Spirit is love, joy, peace, patience, kindness, goodness, faithfulness,…

Galatians 5:19 & 22

Let me make three quick observations.

First, the items listed are intended to be heard together not separately. The author is trying to create an overall impression by heaping up qualities, whether good or bad. So instead of beginning with a dissection of the list's individual terms, ask: what is the list's big picture?

Second, the lists are usually suggestive and are not intended to be all-inclusive. It's not wise to treat them as if they are complete.

For example, there are three places in the New Testament letters that mention the gifts of the spirit and each is different than the other. Apparently, Paul never tried to list every possible gift in any of his writings. That makes sense to me. How long would it take to list all the skills, talents, and abilities evident in the people just in this room? Do you think that spiritual gifts are any less diverse? I don't think so!

Third, the order of the vices/virtues in the list is sometimes important, so pay attention. Sometimes, the author is building to a climax. Sometimes he is putting a "bookend" on each end of the list with two important ideas.

Chiasm

One of the most overlooked methods is a chiasm. It's often overlooked because we aren't all that familiar with the concept in our writings. In the writings of the ancient world and particularly in among the Hebrew, Greek, and Roman cultures it was something that people looked for and enjoyed in all kinds of writing.

This rhetorical tool is simply the arrangement of ideas to form a mirroring pattern. Each section in a text matches a later corresponding section. For example, look at the structure in Ephesians 2:1-10

A. Because we walked in our sins (2:1, 2a),
    B. And the devil was at work within us (2:2b),
        C. God's wrath was coming because of our deeds (2:3).
            D. But because God is rich in mercy (2:4),
                E. We are made alive with Christ (2:5a).
                    F. By grace we have been saved (2:5b).
                E. We are raised up with Christ (2:6),
            D. Because God is rich in grace (2:7).
        C. God's gift came, not because of our deeds (2:8, 9).
    B. Now God is at work within us (2:10a),
A. So we walk in good works (2:10b).

Ephesians 2:1-10

Ancients noticed and enjoyed chiasm much as we notice and enjoy Dr. Seuss or if you are a bit more sophisticated, Robert Frost.

For us, rhyming makes something easier to remember and often gives us appreciation that the writer thought carefully when constructing his material . . . Readers in Paul's day viewed chiasm the same way.

Here's the important thing to remember about chiasm: Whereas we usually put something first or last for emphasis, the ancients put the emphasis in the middle. Look at the mirroring in the Ephesians 2:1-10 passage and notice the big idea in the middle.

Metaphor

For no one can lay a foundation other than that which is laid, which is Jesus Christ.

1 Corinthians 3:11

...built on the foundation of the apostles and prophets, Christ Jesus himself being the cornerstone...

Ephesians 2:20

We are probably most familiar with this last "preacher's tool." The New Testament letters read like picture books, as the images flow constantly from the writers' pens.

The church is pictured as a bride, a body, and a flock of sheep. We did a whole series of teachings last fall on these matters.

The Christian life is pictured as a race, a battle, and a farm.

But here's a key principle: metaphors are flexible. They don't always mean the same thing in different places.

In 1 Corinthians 3:11, Paul says the church's foundation is Jesus Christ, but in Ephesians 2:20, Paul says the church's foundation is the apostles and prophets, while Jesus is the cornerstone.

So don't assume you know what a metaphor means because of its use elsewhere. Paul got creative with his metaphorical references, so check the context every time.

The NT Letters by Author

The Letters by Author and by Audience

Pauline Letters

Church Letters	Personal Letters
Romans	1 & 2 Timothy
1 & 2 Corinthians	Titus
Galatians	Philemon
Ephesians	
Philippians	Hebrews
Colossians	
1 7 2 Thessalonians	

Apostles Letters

General Letters

James
1 & 2 Peter
1, 2, & 3 John
Jude

Where to Begin Depends on What You Need

Understanding Salvation – Romans or Ephesians
Relational and Spiritual Growth in the Church –
Corinthians
Freedom from the OT Law – Galatians
Difference between OT and NT Covenants – Hebrews
Church Leadership – Timothy and Titus
The power of God's Love – John
The way of Faith – Peter

Action Steps

- ❑ Repent and be baptized…
- ❑ Start reading one of the epistles
- ❑ Pray for understanding
- ❑ Pray for an opportunity to share your faith

Discussion Questions

1. Which of the letters is your favorite and which is the most challenging to you? (And why!)

2. Read 1 Timothy 1:17. Are you familiar with other scriptures that are made into songs today or were in the early church?

3. Read Ephesians 6:1-10. What are the household rules presented here? How do they affect the impact of the gospel

4. Read the Vice List in 1 Timothy 1:9-10. Now, compare this list with the Ten Commandments in Exodus 20:6. What do you notice?

5. A chiasm is the arrangement of ideas to form a mirroring pattern. Can you detect the chiasm in Romans 10:9-10?

6. The NT letters are full of metaphors. Can you think of examples of metaphors for the church in the letters? What about the Christian life?

7. What does Jesus want you to do differently this week?

APOCALYPTIC LITERATURE

We've been looking at the big picture of the Bible, providing some context to the different writings in the Bible so that we can better understand them. We started with the Old Testament books of history, books of prophecy, and the wisdom literature, then we moved to the New Testament biographies, history, and letters.

The final chapter is a type of writing in the Bible called apocalyptic literature. This section in the New Testament is made up of only one book: the book of Revelation.

The book of Revelation provokes different reactions in us. Its fantastic language, filled with beasts and dragons and angels, often causes us to wonder what real practical use it has for our lives, which often just results in us ignoring it. We just don't read it.

Yet we also recognize that there's something mystical and powerful and important about its message, so we desire to understand it. Sometimes we take that so far that we obsess about its symbols and language and attempt to interpret its messages.

Even the secular world is fascinated by the contents of Revelation. Every year, movies come out based on themes from the book of Revelation, with titles like "The Omen," "The

Seventh Sign", "The Prophecy," and "Legion." (I think Christopher Walken was in every one of those...)

I think in everyone, though, is a basic desire, "Help me understand it!" Our goal today, as with the rest of this series, is to provide some context that will help us better understand it when we read it.

Disclaimer – If you're anticipating that I'm going to tell you that the anti-Christ is indeed Nancy Pelosi, Bill Gates, President Obama, the Pope, or Justin Bieber, you're probably going to be disappointed.

Initial Matters

First of all, this is very important: The title Revelation is singular! It's not Revelations, it's Revelation. Now we can move on to more trivial matters.

The title Revelation is from the Greek word "apokalupsis", meaning "disclosure" or "unveiling." It describes an unveiling of what is hidden to the reader, maybe because it's in another realm, or to come in the future. Revelation in the Bible deals with the end times. Its Greek title, Apocalypse, has now, in English, come to describe the end of the world. But in the context of this book of the Bible, it was an unveiling, a lifting of the curtain, a revelation.

In verse 9 of the first chapter, the writer is identified: "I, John, your brother and companion in the suffering and kingdom and patient endurance that are ours in Jesus, was on the island of Patmos because of the word of God and the testimony of Jesus." Traditional interpretation is that he was sent to Patmos to live in exile because of his belief and faith in Jesus.

There are two main ideas for when Revelation was written, but the most widely accepted was that it was written around 95 AD.

At that time, the Southern Kingdom of Judah has since developed into the territory of Judea. Had been ruled by the Babylonians, Persians, Egyptians, Greeks, and is now a part of the Roman Empire, subject to its laws and commands. Christians are living in Judea and around the Roman Empire.

At different times in the first century, persecution against Christians by the Roman authorities varied. At some points there was an active torturing and killing of Christians by the Roman government in horrific way. Historical writers mention Christians being forced to wear animal skins and being torn apart by dogs, or Christians being burned alive to provide illumination at night. They suffered horrible things.

At other times, the official stance toward Christians was the same as other religious groups and cults, the Roman Empire tolerated them as long as they didn't cause trouble. There was, though, often a pressure to acknowledge the divinity of the emperor, which of course to Christians, was unacceptable, as they worshiped no Lord but Jesus. So keep that picture in mind of the original readers of this work: believers who are dealing with these kinds of pressures.

What's in the book of Revelation?

The book opens with John seeing a vision of Jesus in all his glory, telling him to write down what he is about to see.

Chapters 2-3 are probably the most recognizable to us, because they are the easiest to understand. They contain letters to seven individual churches around Western Asia, reminding them to stay faithful to Jesus.

Chapters 4-20 are a series of events taking place in the heavenly realm. They lay out this picture of God's authority and his power to defeat evil. It's often arranged in symbolic packages of seven, and interspersed with side stories.

Finally, chapters 21-22 close out the book by describing the restoration of God's kingdom and it paints this incredible picture of heaven and what his reign will be like.

Ok, so the question that we're asking today is how do we read and understand it?

When we read that there will be two witnesses to God who will be killed and lay in the street for three and a half days, then

God's breath will cause them to stand back up, how do we understand that?

When we read that a mark of a beast will be put on everyone's right hand or forehead, and the number of the beast is 666, how do we interpret that? Well, I'm not going to tell you!

Common Approaches to the Book of Revelation

All of these approaches focus on whether it predicts the future or not. Depending on your view this affects how you interpret the content.

- **Preterist** Approach, in which Revelation mostly refers to the events of 1st century; it was not meant to predict or speak of the distant future, but to speak to the audience to which it was written, and encourage them. So, with this view, people saw in the symbols the evil of the Roman Empire, and God's conquest over it, and the fulfillment of the events in the 1st century. One of the issues with this view if fully accepted, however, is that this also resulted in a belief that even the return and reign of Jesus as described in Revelation had already happened in the 1st century!

- **Historical** Approach, which basically sees Revelation as a broad view of history; so the events of Revelation progressed throughout the history of the world. They located specific texts with specific events throughout history. This was a common interpretation with the leaders of the Protestant Reformation: John Calvin, Martin Luther. Their movement was a reaction against what they saw as the evil of the Catholic Church, and so they interpreted the Antichrist who rose up in opposition to God's sovereignty as the Pope. This is probably the least common approach today.

- **Symbolic** Approach, which holds that Revelation does not refer to actual people or events, but is an allegory of the spiritual path and the ongoing struggle between good and evil. The events and figures are just symbols and metaphors, like "The Pilgrim's Progress," or "The Chronicles of Narnia."

- **Futurist** Approach, which believes that Revelation describes very specific future events (mainly at the end of the world) that will happen in a specific timeframe that the book seems to lay out. It sounds pretty clear-cut, but unfortunately it's not, because based on how the events are interpreted, it's produced a wide variety of views within the futurist approach. But, this is one of the most popular ways to look at Revelation today, almost to the point where it's accepted as fact by most Christians because they don't know any other way. Its popularity is evidenced by the Left Behind books, Harold Camping's predictions, etc. The doctrine of the rapture comes from reading Revelation with this view, the idea of Jesus reigning on earth for 1,000 years comes from this view.

And of course, there are numerous other ways throughout history that people have attempted to interpret the book of Revelation, and even combinations of these. Again, it speaks to that desire we have…help me understand it!

How I Read Revelation

I'll be honest with you, I can understand the appeal of each of these approaches, but at the same time, I have issues with each one of them. I thought I'd share with you how I approach it, and hopefully it will help you as you read the book of Revelation.

I can't read the book of Revelation without applying the same principles to it that I apply to every other section of the Bible, and that affects my interpretation.

The first question I ask when reading the Bible is "what type of writing is the book I'm in?" That's the first thing I remember when I read Paul's letters, or the history in Genesis, or the Gospels. This is especially important when it comes to the book of Revelation so that we do not misunderstand it.

Revelation belongs to a specific genre of Jewish writing called apocalyptic literature existing in the time period around 200 BC to 100 AD. Like any other genre of literature, it had consistent characteristics:

a. In apocalyptic literature, a secret revelation is being given to a seer or prophet through some type of mediator, often an angel, who acts as a guide and interpreter. This revelation is usually unveiled through a dream, vision, or the seer being transported to a divine realm.

b. The revelation usually consists of a variety of symbols, including animals, numbers, stars and moon, etc.

c. The purpose for apocalyptic literature was this: to explain to the Jewish people why they, who were supposed to be God's chosen people, were living as subjects and suffering under an earthly pagan government. The answer that was given was that Satan was now controlling the kingdoms of the world, but that God was in charge of history, and would soon intervene by sending the Messiah to the earth, conquering evil, bringing judgment and justice, and restoring his kingdom as sovereign over all.

d. The goal of the apocalyptic literature was not to point toward <u>when</u> and <u>how</u> this would happen, but that it <u>would</u> happen, and how that affected how the readers should then live. The writers weren't really interested in speculating about the end times, that wouldn't have any meaning to their readers who were suffering. They were interested in the here and now, and the encouragement and hope that the promise of the end times would bring.

John, through the inspiration of God, takes this genre of literature, and appropriates it for his purposes. Only, instead of Jews suffering under foreign governments, he addresses it to Christians who are suffering persecution under foreign governments. With the understanding that Jesus was the hoped-for Messiah who had already come, John points to the end of days with a promise that God is in control of the ultimate path of history, and one day soon Jesus will return with judgment, a final dealing with evil, and the restoration of his kingdom as sovereign over all.

Can you see what this would have meant to the original readers of Revelation, and how this would have been an encouragement to stay faithful in the midst of their friends and family members being killed for their belief in Christ?

With an understanding of this genre of apocalyptic literature, treating Revelation the same way as I treat other books of the Bible, I read it with a view that Revelation was written in a very specific style and for a very specific purpose, to communicate a specific message to a specific people.

This is why I have a resistance to the futuristic approach to Revelation so common today. It causes us to read it in ways that weren't intended and negates the meaning it originally had. We are just so unfamiliar with apocalyptic literature and its fantastic language of beasts, angels, prostitutes, and dragons, that I think we just naturally assume it fits our pictures of the end times, which are mystical and mysterious. And then it results in us interpreting things in ways that they weren't meant to.

So symbols such as a beast with seven heads, and the number 666, for example, held meaning recognized by its first century readers, and helped to convey that idea of encouragement in the present.

It was not meant to give us clues that we're to use to interpret the future; it was intended to encourage the reader that the future was known by and directed by God.

This is what gives the book timeless value - for readers throughout history and even today.

By trying to snatch these images out of their first-century context and use them for our purposes and applying them to the end times, it has some consequences: 1) we'll be wrong. Just look at Harold Camping and scores of others who have tried. 2) We'll miss out on what the message of Revelation means for us right now, and that is this:

1. There is a bigger story going on behind the scenes; our struggle is not against flesh and blood. This is an unveiling of things we cannot see.

2. There is a definite relationship between the life that now is and the life to come. There is encouragement to stay faithful in persecution. Don't allow yourself to be assimilated into the culture of the country in which you live.

3. God is triumphant; his kingdom is sovereign and is coming, along with restoration of all that was lost in the fall of mankind.

Focusing on those things makes Revelation extremely applicable and practical to us as believers today.

Action Steps

- ❏ Read the book of Revelation in one sitting.
- ❏ Read a commentary or more in-depth resource on Revelation.
- ❏ Read the book of Revelation again!
- ❏ Join a group that is studying the Bible.
- ❏ Start a regular Bible reading plan.

Discussion Questions

1. Have you ever read the book of Revelation completely? What is your general impression of the book?

2. Consider the four ways to read the book of Revelation. Which do you lean toward and why?

   a. Preterist: Limited to the Apostolic age
   b. Historical: Fulfilled in modern history
   c. Symbolic: An allegory of the spiritual path
   d. Futurist: Describes the end of the world in future events

3. Harold Camping predicted the end of the world (May 21 and then October 21, 2011.) Read Matthew 24:36. Why do we need to be careful about predictions?

4. What does Revelation teach you about Jesus and what you need to do with your life?

ABOUT THE AUTHORS

Rick Stacy: Rick Stacy came to Meridian Christian Church in 1998 after starting churches in Beavercreek, Ohio (1986) and in Marquette, MI (1977). He and his wife, Donna, have been serving in the ministry since they graduated from Great Lakes Christian College in 1973. Rick has a Bachelor of Religious Education degree from Great Lakes Christian College and a Masters of Practical Ministry degree from Kentucky Christian College. They both work together to help people build relationships with one another and with God.

Jamie Wetzel: Jamie Wetzel is the Administrative Minister, overseeing the organizational administration of Meridian Christian Church. He and his wife Julie have worked with MCC since 1996. Jamie graduated from Great Lakes Christian College in 1998 and completed his Masters degree from Cincinnati Bible Seminary in 2002.

Made in the USA
Middletown, DE
23 April 2015